I Cried Out and He Heard Me

Emma Lee Martin

Copyright © 2012 Emma Lee Martin

All rights reserved.

ISBN: 0615355110
ISBN-13: 978-0615355115
Library of Congress Control Number: 2011942353

DEDICATION

This book of poetry is dedicated to God. He gave me the courage to write and complete this book. God allowed me to obtain my answers to the questions regarding life trials and tribulations by means of going through the wilderness.

CONTENTS

Acknowledgments i

A BIG FISH IN A SMALL POND	1		14
A CHILD RUNNING WILD	2		15
A MESSAGE TO THE YOUNG	3		16
ACCEPTANCE	4		17
ANGER	5		18
AUTHORITY OF OWN LIFE	6		19
BETRAYAL	7		20
BLIND BY JUSTICE	8		21
BLOOD THICKER THAN WATER	9		22
BROKEN HEARTED	10		23
CAN YOU HANDLE THE TRUTH?	11		24
CASTING PEARLS TO SWINE	12		25
CAVIAR APPETITE	13		26
CHARACTER ASSASSINATION	14		27
CIRCLE OF INFLUENCES	15		28
CONSUMED WITH GRIEF	16		29
CONTROL YOURSELF	17		30
COPING WITH LIFE	18		31
COURAGE	19		32

DECEPTION 20	33
DEMOCRACY 21	34
DENIAL 22	35
DO NOT BLAME IT ON ME! 23	36
DO NOT SAY A WORD 24	37
DOUBLE LIFE 25	38
DREAM KILLERS 26	39
DRUGS ARE SELF DESTRUCTION 27	40
EMBRACING WHO AND WHERE YOU ARE 28	41
EVIL LURKING AT MY DOOR 29	42
EXPECTATIONS MISUNDERSTOOD 30	43
EXPERIMENT 31	44
FALSE FACES 32	45
FAMILY 33	46
FINDING MY WAY IN THE UNIVERSE 34	47
FRAGILE HEART 35	48
FREEDOM 36	49
FRIENDSHIP 37	50
GENERATIONAL CURSE 38	51
HATER 39	52
HAUNTED BY MY PAST 40	53
HOW COULD IT BE? 41	54
HUMAN SHIELD 42	55

HUMANITY	43
HUMILIATION	44
I AM HAPPY IN MY SKIN	45
I CRIED OUT AND HE HEARD ME	46
I FORGIVE YOU	47
I HAD TO BE MYSELF	48
IDENTITY CRISIS	49
IDLE MIND	50
IMMATURE	51
IMPERFECTION	52
INSTITUTIONALIZED MENTALLY	53
JOY-JUST OFFER YOURSELF	54
LEECHES	55
LIE	56
LIFE	57
LIFELESS	58
LEAVING AMERICA	59
LIVING IN A WORLD OF CONFUSION	60
LIVING WITH THE ENEMIES	61
LOYALTY	62
MAKING THE RIGHT DECISION	63
MIND GAMES	64
MISERABLE WITHIN ONESELF	65

56
57
58
59
60
61
62
63
64
65
66
67
68
69
70
71
72
73
74
75
76
77
78

MONEY CANNOT BUY LOVE	66	79
MULTIPLE PERSONALITIES	67	80
MY LAST BREATH	68	81
MY SOUL DELIVERED FROM DEATH	69	82
NO SENSE OF DIRECTION	70	83
OPTIMISTIC	71	84
PAIN-Penetrating Anger in Negativity	72	85
PEACE	73	86
PESSIMISM	74	87
POOR IS A STATE OF MIND	75	88
PRIDE	76	89
RACISM	77	90
RESPECT	78	91
RICH IN SPIRIT	79	92
SACRIFICE	80	93
SECRET ENEMIES	81	94
SELF-ABSORBED	82	95
SELF EXAMINATION	83	96
SELF-HATRED FREEWILL	84	97
SELF INFLICTED NARCOTIC (SIN)	85	98
SELF PORTRAIT OF LOVE	86	99
SEVENTH CHILD	87	100
SEX-SELF EXPOSED XXX	88	101

SHATTERED DREAMS	89	102
SHELTERED	90	103
SHOCK AND AW	91	104
SILENT ADVERSARIES	92	105
SPIRITUAL DARKNESS	93	106
STRENGTH THROUGH FAITH	94	107
SUFFERING IN SILENCE	95	108
THE BRIGHT LIGHT	96	109
THE PAIN WILL STOP ONE DAY	97	110
THIEVES	98	111
TRAGEDY AFTER TRAGEDY	99	112
TRUST	100	113
TRUTH	101	114
UNITY	102	115
		116

VINDICTIVE SOULS	103	116
VISION	104	117
WAR IN THE HEART	105	118
WHAT CLAN WAS I BORN IN?	106	119
WHERE I AM, IS NOT WHO I AM	107	120
WHO ARE THEY REALLY?	108	121
WHY DID I SURVIVE?	109	122
WISDOM WASTED	110	123
WOLVES IN SHEEP CLOTHING	111	124
WORDS SMOOTHER THAN BUTTER	112	125

ACKNOWLEDGMENTS

Earth Tone Publishing
Copyright@2012 by Emma Lee Martin
All Rights Reserved
Book Cover by Shane Poteete with Built Creative
Photography by Portrait Innovations

1 A BIG FISH IN A SMALL POND

I was a big fish in a small pond.
They waved a magic wand.
I built a wall.
God protected me from them all.
They were singing that same old song.
They did not care about right or wrong.
All my dreams were shattered.
All of them scattered.
I was the smartest in my group.
All they wanted was my loot.
They s stopped dreaming.
All of them were screaming.
They were so corrupt and could not see.
They were so focused on me.
God searches the heart.
God shifted the guard from a big fish in a small pond.

2 A CHILD RUNNING WILD

I was a child running wild.
I would never have a smile.
My heart was cold as ice.
Everyone I encountered was not very nice.
I was so naive.
I could not achieve, nor did I believe.
No one ever took the time to share God's love with me.
It caused me not to see, what I could be.
It came a time in my life that I had to make a choice.
It was to listen to God's still voice.
God called my name.
I thought I was going insane.
It did not cause me any harm.
God welcomed me with open arms.
I thank God for giving me a second chance.
God brought me out of every circumstance.
I told God; I will tell the world what he did for me.
God has truly set me free.

3 A MESSAGE TO THE YOUNG

If a person does not have it in his or her heart;
he or she is not a true believer in GOD.
People should leave other business alone.
They will be here after you are gone.
If they were a true friend, they would not tell you anything
that would do you in.
We as human beings centered our lives on material things.
When GOD calls your name then it is your turn to go under his wings.
Two wrongs do not make it right.
Ask GOD and he shall show you the light.
Have faith and believe in yourself, and you can conquer all.
Mostly you must believe in GOD.
The life you live! Is the life you die!
I hope all young people do not think this is a game.
If they do not stop the madness in the streets, they will end up the same.
Like my baby sister dead
In loving memory of Evelyn

4 ACCEPTANCE

It is ok not to be accepted by others.
They were yearning for their father or mother.
If I must be accepted by doing this or that;
I have not seen anything yet.
The mind is the most precious gift to human beings.
God is the only one who is seeing.
I had to put away my pride.
My mind possesses too much greatness inside.
One must learn to reflect on the positive.
God is the only one who allows us to live.
Life greatest lesson is to know.
God will never leave me at the door.
God advised the storm would not last.
I had to leave negative people in the past.
I did not allow people or possessions to label me.
God set me free.
One must take pleasure in what he or she does.
God sent true acceptance from above.
Some of them do not have a clue.
I learned to be true to me not you.
Courage comes from doing what is right. I had to fight.
Today is today and not tomorrow.
God delivered me from all my sorrows.
The mind does one thing, but the heart says everything.
You must be confident in who you are.
This will help you get very far.
God will give me my star.
God accepts you as you are.

5 ANGER

Anger steals.
Anger has cheap thrills.
Anger is an emotional roller coaster ride.
Anger is bitterness kept inside.
Anger turns your smile upside down.
Anger makes you act like a clown.
Anger is a silent killer.
Anger makes you feel bitter.
Anger controls your thought process.
Anger keeps you from obtaining success.
Anger separated families.
Anger divided countries.
Anger kills without a cause.
Anger separates us from the will of GOD.
Anger is not here to stay.
Ask GOD and he will show you the way.
Do not be angry about a person's life!
Ask God to remove the strife.

6 AUTHORITY OF OWN LIFE

Power placed in the wrong hand.
It can swift you like sand.
I tried to see the best in all human beings.
I could not believe what my eyes were seeing.
I had to be careful who I trust.
Evil comes to destroy all of us.
I tried to control my life.
It created nothing but strife.
God has paid the price.
I had to learn.
I did not want to be burned.
God's love kept me from making the wrong turn.
God's says I did not earn.
It comes from no other.
God removed the cover.
I respect it.
God displayed it.
It was a gift from God.
I gave him my heart.
God has all authority.
God gives me his royalty.

7 BETRAYAL

Betrayal entered my life.
Betrayal created all kind of strife.
You, I thought I could trust.
Betrayal came between us.
You laugh in my face.
All the time you were trying to take my place.
What you did in the night.
God revealed to me the light.
It was up to me: if I wanted to see.
You know who you are.
You did not get very far.
Betrayal, I forgive you.
Betrayal will never be true.
No, matter what you do.
Betrayal, I want to thank you for revealing your identity.
If it was not for you, I would not be ushered into my destiny.

8 BLINDS BY JUSTICE

Justice is so blind. Your life can be over in a drop of a dime.
10 20 Life is a new time.
Justice is so blind. Now the judges are on prime time.
Human's deficiencies are displayed for the world to see.
It could be my sister, brother, or even me.
Justice does discriminate they do not give a fair trial.
Justice wants them in their judicial system for a while.
They are treated like animals.
Some of the crimes do not compensate the time.
I do admit we need to take criminals off the street.
We need to put officer friendly back on the beat.
We took God out of the schools.
Kids have their own tools.
Justice is looking like a fool.
We must change policies and procedures.
Our country will end up under seizure.
They talk about prison sentences as if it is a social event.
God was not in it.
It is so sad what we reduced humankind to.
God is the only one who can guide us through.

9 BLOOD THICKER THAN WATER

How could someone be hated by her sisters and brothers?
Strangers showed me more love than my kin
Little did they know they were committing a sin.
God is love, but they hated me so much.
They could not embrace my simple touch.
I became a reflection of what they could be.
All they did was hate on me.
They could not see.
I was not the one. They could not make it without his only son.
They were so busy making false accusations.
They could not see my transformation.
There was so many of them I lost count. They made me shout.
A friend sticks closer than a brother is so true. They do not have a clue.
They do not stick together like glue.
They are like clay. They do not know what to say.
They need to be shaped and molded, but that is not my job.
It must come from God.
They allowed jealousy to consume them so bad.
They are wishing they had what I had.
Courage is to move on.
When everyone has done you wrong or died and left you alone.
I did not know the hatred was so deep; until one day, God gave me a peep.
It was the most devastating thing to experience.
Blood is supposed to be thicker than water.
They would not even lend me a quarter.
I tried to make sense of all this madness.
It brought me nothing but sadness.
I let them all go and maybe one day they will know.
I tried to help them grow into love.
That was sent from heaven above.

10 BROKEN HEARTED

I was broken hearted.
Every emotion was discarded.
I had given my entire being.
None of them could be seeing.
I could not predict what was to come.
My heart was pierced by everyone.
God prevented me from being on the run.
God sent his only son.
My heart was so fragile.
They were worshiping idles.
The pain lasted for a while.
It removed my smile.
God said do not worry my child.
I will mend your broken heart.
Just give me a minute to get started.
I will put every vessel back in place.
I will remove the disgrace from your face.
God told me so. The blood will flow very slow.
I will get my fragile heart back.
It will be fully in tack.
I had to get his word for myself.
God embraced on my behalf.

11 CAN YOU HANDLE THE TRUTH?

My truth sets me free.
God protected me from the enemy.
It started with my youth.
This is my truth.
My truth was surrounded by so many negative images.
God removed the blemishes.
I tried to block it out of my mind.
I pondered on it all the time.
My truth is no one wakes up and says.
I want to be a junkie today.
God says we must pray.
I did not ask to grow up in a dysfunctional environment.
Some of them did not see retirement.
I was torn between two evils.
I tried to blame it on the devils.
I did pursue my endeavors. I was very clever.
I am a human being.
Things did not appear, as they seem.
I could not give up on my dreams.
I used drugs and alcohol to hide the pain.
I used humans to cover shame.
God did not allow it to drive me insane.
I ran for so many years. God wiped away my tears.
I embraced my reality. I accepted the causalities.
This is my truth. What is your truth?
Can you handle the truth?

12 CASTING PEARLS TO SWINE

God gave me so many rhythms and rhymes.
I am gifted casting my pearls to swine.
It did not cost me a dime.
They could not handle what God had given me.
God did not let them see.
They tried to throw me under the bus.
God was the only one I could trust.
In their mind, they thought it was their time.
God searched their hearts.
God did not get very far.
He could not trust them with his treasures.
They could never measure.
They were so wicked inside.
God could not guide.
They were wondering why me and not them.
God told them they were not a gem.
God had seen so much corruption from within.
God could not dwell there.
They thought it was not fair.
I told them if they did what I did.
God would give them a gig.
They did not want to listen.
I heard them whistling.
I wish it was me; casting my pearls into the sea.

13 CAVIAR APPETITE

This was my reality.
I was hanging out with the ghetto mentality.
I experienced this life at an early age.
Little did I know I would end up in a cage?
I look as though I came out of an upscale magazine.
Things did not appear, as they seem.
The outside looked extremely clean.
The inside was incredibly mean.
I played the part very well.
Little did I know I was going to hell?
I could not get rid of the ghetto mindset.
Money and power made everyone want to chat.
God had not stepped in yet.
I had all the finer things in life.
I was not fit to be anyone's wife.
I made it all about me.
I was strong and tall as a tree.
God stepped in and set me free.

14 CHARACTER ASSASSINATION

The adversaries hate what they see.
They wanted to be me.
They lash out with false accusations. It gives them a fake sensation.
I had done all that I could. I had taken assignments no one would.
No, matter what I did. It was never good enough.
They had thrown me under the bus.
God knows I did my best. God says it was only a test.
My character removed evil with good.
God opened doors no one could.
The wicked were prowling at my door.
Evil was trying to make a score.
God said no more.
It does not matter what I did in my head.
The enemy thought I was dead.
It is what resides in my heart.
That is something that comes from God.
I tried to find good in everyone.
The enemy put me on the run.
I used to seek others approval a long time ago.
God tells me everything I need to know.
I sought his face. They could not take my place.
It gives me a piece of mind.
It did not cost me a dime.
I know who has my back, and not place my character under attack.

15 CIRCLES OF INFLUENCES

Everyone claimed to be a connection.
God was the only one with affection.
It did not matter what they were doing.
I thought I had a circle of influence:
However, their situations were worse than mine.
God told me not to cast my pearls to swine.
Things were not as it seemed.
It made me scream.
I did not like how I was treated.
God was all I needed.
God removed them who had their hidden agenda.
God did not allow them to put me under.
He left them wondering.
How did she do this or that?
God word does not lie and there is not a catch.
I will never doubt what God can do for me.
God sets me free.

16 CONSUMED WITH GRIEF

I was consumed with grief.
This was my belief.
Everywhere I went. There was a tragedy.
I had to come up with a new strategy.
I thought this was the way of life.
Grief cuts like a knife.
When would it ever stop?
God was the one I sought.
God changed my thoughts.
I had to rethink twice.
God did not roll the dice.
Someone had to pay the price.
It was all a sacrifice.
For me to live, someone had to die.
This is my truth and not a lie.
It did not matter how or when they died.
God was the only one on my side.

17 CONTROL YOURSELF

I learned to control myself.
I was not seeking control over anyone else.
It was issued plaguing my past.
It did not last.
I looked beyond my being.
God was the one seeing.
I had taken control.
I eliminated those who treated me cold.
Power struggles come with a price.
They were not very nice.
Some of them were cold as ice.
God let me see.
He could manage my life better than me.
I headed down the wrong path.
My enemies had begun to laugh.
My life was shattered glass.
God showed me it would not last.
I know at the end of the day.
God has the last say.

18 COPING WITH LIFE

Coping with life can be hard to do.
When no one loves you.
I had to be true to me not you.
Love does not have to be family or friends.
I opened my heart and let God in.
The world is full of sins.
God knows the beginning and the end.
God did not let me carry the burden alone.
I believed in God and he made me strong.
Life does not come with instructions.
I trusted God's directions.
It was not what I wanted to hear.
God removed the fear.
God wiped away every tear.
God was always near.

19 COURAGE

Courage is doing what is not popular.
God accepts you as you are.
The results are priceless.
I got everything off my chest.
God allows me to do my best. God will handle the rest.
God says it is only a test.
Courage faces the wicked. God gives a free ticket.
Courage did not utter a sound.
God turns the enemy plan upside down.
Daring is waiting on God.
It is keeping a pure heart.
I did not have the nerve to serve.
I was pushed to the curve.
No matter what hand life had dealt me.
God and his word set me free.
God did not give me a spirit of fear.
God was always near.
God removed all my tears.
That was plaguing me for so many years.
God gave me the strength to be brave.
I am no longer anyone's slave.
I thank God I am saved.
Courage removed obstacles that came in my path.
God has the last laugh.
Courage is boldness that surpasses all understanding.
God kept me standing and guided me with a perfect landing.

20 DECEPTION

If you practice what you, preach.
It would not be deceit.
I was looking at life with a spiritual eye.
I was seeking the truth and not living a lie.
Deception I know your name.
I experienced an extraordinary change.
The world will never be the same.
People are dying every day.
For what someone else had to say.
Deception builds on lies and deceit.
Deception is trying to see who else it can cheat.
Deception always expresses envy.
Do not feel that way towards me!
I am just a human being trying to make it.
Do not be another one trying to take it!
The enemy comes to kill, steal, and destroy.
Stop letting him play you like a toy!
Deception comes in different forms, shapes, and styles.
Deception hangs in your life for a while.
I did not know how to cope.
I asked GOD to show me the rope.

21 DEMOCRACY

Democracy is life, liberty and the pursuit of happiness.
I tried that concept, but experience sadness.
I vote for a person to represent me the people.
The past leadership had their hidden agendas.
It left this country owing trillions of dollars.
I accepted our new president.
He represents what America is supposed to be.
Americans shed blood to set us free.
We should not be judged by the color of our skin.
He has an honest spirit within.
We need to view what he has to offer us and the world.
God blessed him with a wife and two beautiful girls.
I do not see our new president as my messiah.
I am tired of all the liars.
America is ready for change. We are tired of doing the same old thing.
If we want different results, we need to get rid of the cults.
I did not vote for our President because he is black.
I voted because he represents what this country lack.
President Obama represents what all humankind should have integrity.
He is not trying to cut a deal for his friends or family.
He stands tall as a tree. He cares for all of humankind and including me.
I think we need to show our President some respect.
His eight years are not over yet.
Now, we wonder why we get so much slack.
We want other countries to follow our lead.
Some Americans lost their way due to greed.

22 DENIAL

I was in denial about certain things in my life.
Denial cut my heart like a knife.
I could not make it go away.
God revealed it to me every day.
I was very defiant.
Denial made me its next client.
I faced the truth.
It dated back to my youth.
God made it perfectly clear.
He would always be near.
It was the most difficult thing I had to do.
I had to face the person in the mirror and be true.
No matter where I go.
Denial took over the show.
I was denied promotions on my job.
God advised me not to sob.
I was denounced by my friends and family.
God rescued me from my calamities.
Denial does not care what anyone says.
I followed God ways.
God saved me in these last evil days.

23 DO NOT BLAME IT ON ME!

Do not blame it on me!
I am a product of what I see.
I did not reach my destiny.
I am waiting on the Trinity.
I am procrastinating.
I am so busy dating.
I do not have a job or skills.
I seek cheap thrills.
I wasted my talents and gifts.
The times shift.
I was consumed by the idiot box.
I am trapped like a fox.
I think society owes me something.
I chose not to do anything.
I allowed this to happen to me.
Now I am singing do not blame it on me.
I get one shot at life: before I die.
I can believe the truth or the lie.
Life is not easy stop trying to live cheesy.
I am responsible for my life after a certain age.
The wrong choices I could end up in a cage.
One must lead by example for the little ones.
The parents are the role models, not the famous ones.
Children live by what they see.
Do not let the child sing do not blame it on me.

24 DO NOT SAY A WORD

I was in the presence of my enemies.
God made me fall on my knees.
God told me not to say a word.
He would use his sword.
The enemy could not read my mind.
I was wasting my time.
It did not cost me a dime.
I never saw so many corrupt souls.
They were sold.
This is what I was told.
The enemy did not know what I was thinking.
It helped the plots to start shrinking.
It did not matter if it was a man or a woman.
God destroyed their plan.
God exposed everything they tried to do.
God was always true.
It made them feel blue.
God let me see.
They tried to destroy me.
They were living in the past.
God showed me it would not last.
Silence is the number one killer.
It keeps you from cheap thrillers.
God could not do it without me.
God has set me free.

25 DOUBLE LIFE

He was living a double life.
It created all type of strife.
I thought I knew who he was.
I made him my only love.
I let people think what they wanted.
I was being hunted.
I tried to be transparent.
It was very apparent.
They did not care.
I tried to share.
They wanted what I had.
It was very sad.
I wish I had my dad.
I would be very glad.
There was nothing wrong with what I was doing in my eyes.
God made me realize.
I had to get him out of my life.
I could never be his wife.
I was chastised.
God was the only one on my side.

26 DREAM KILLERS

Some people are dream killers.
They are cheap thrillers.
They told me that I have mine.
You need to get yours.
Dream killers can rob your soul.
Some of them misplaced their dreams.
Things for them do not appear, as it seems.
It is the closest one to you.
They cannot be happy for you nor be true.
Dream killers were trying to destroy my goals.
They were so cold.
They lashed out.
They tried to fill my mind with doubt.
They were crushed by past pains and hurts.
They treated me like dirt.
No, matter what they did or said.
I was not afraid.
God would guide me through: if I did not give up.
Dream killers will be the first to show up.
Success comes with a price.
God has paid with his son's life.

27 DRUGS ARE SELF DESTRUCTION

Drugs are the number one killer.
It gives the impression of a powerful thriller.
It kills your friends and family.
Some of them lost their sanity.
Drugs divided countries.
Drugs are the number one enemy.
This epidemic affects all walks of life.
It could cripple your husband or wife.
Those who can afford treatment hide in centers.
The poor walks the street: because they cannot afford to enter.
Drugs are not only on a local level. It is stronger than any devil.
What do you do when it gets worse?
Pray to God to remove this evil curse.
If you ever pass a person on the streets, do not criticize him or her.
It could be your brother or sister.
No one wakes up and says I want to be a junkie today.
It may be something someone else may say.
It starts out as casual use. Before you know, it has elevated to abuse.
Our children are the future.
Let us not destroy them with this culture!
We should educate them about downers and uppers.
It could be their last supper.
We must guide them to the correct path.
Therefore, they will not make this their craft.
Jail and death are the only way out for some.
Seek God's word and his only begotten son.
You can place righteousness in your heart.
It will never separate you from the will of God.

28 EMBRACING WHO AND WHERE YOU ARE

Embracing who and where you are.
I did not get very far.
Some people think where you are is who you are.
However, little did they know.
God took over the show.
I refused to look back.
God did not give me any slack.
It did not make any sense to fight it.
I was already in it.
It was a long journey.
I thank God I did not have to call an attorney.
Sometimes life can make you bitter.
It shows I am not a quitter.
I am still here.
God was always near.
I did not shed a tear.
I was there for only a minute.
They could never get it.
Who I am is not what I do?
I can be true to me not you.
Embrace who and where you are.
Stop trying to be a star.
Do not let anyone validate who or where you are!

29 EVIL LURKING AT MY DOOR

Evil= Every Vindictive Inner Lie
Evil is so wicked.
Evil made me almost miss my ticket.
Evil is full of transgressions.
Evil tried to take my possessions.
Evil moves around and about.
Evil is seeking clout.
Evil knows who will give in to its temptation.
Evil deprives a person of any sensation.
Evil dangled in my life.
Evil kept up all kinds of strife.
Evil ridiculed me for doing what was right.
Evil tried to make me fight.
Evil did wrong to others.
Evil inherited this from its father or mother.
Evil smiled in my face.
Evil was a disgrace.
Evil tried to take over my place.
Evil comes in different disguises.
God is wise.
Evil tried to hide.
God was on my side.
Evil was lurking at my door.
Evil does not live here anymore.

30 EXPECTATIONS MISUNDERSTOOD

There were so many trying to validate my life.
They were full of strife.
I had to reevaluate myself.
I could not listen to anyone else.
I wanted the finer things.
God has placed me under his wings.
I had to do God's will.
The enemy tried to kill.
The enemy used cheap thrills.
No one could ever give me advice.
God paid the price.
How could you tell me what to do?
You were never true.
Your life is worst than mine.
You cast your treasures to swine.
I was ready to quit.
God said not yet.
My expectations were misunderstood.
God showed me his love like no other could.

31 EXPERIMENT

You were just an experiment.
I did not know when to quit it.
I did not judge you. I was true.
You are in mental bondage.
You tried to hold me hostage.
I know not all men are bad.
It is so sad, but I am glad.
You have revealed yourself to me.
Now I can really see.
You are just another flee on a tree.
You do not deserve to know a woman like me.
You were scorn.
You allowed your heart to be torn.
I gave you the benefit of the doubt.
You were seeking clout.
I had to get it off my chest.
You were only a test.
I thought you changed.
You continued playing games.
I was not going to let you drive me insane.
Tricks are for kids. God had me hid.
I knew all the time. You were not worth a dime.
I let you think you were winning.
You were just sinning.
No matter what you said or done.
I made you think you had won.
God sent his only begotten son.
God can get you on track.
God will not give you any slack.
God will get you through.
God cannot do it without you.

32 FALSE FACES

They tried to put me under.
My God I serve left them wondering.
All their evil failed.
They are sending their soul to hell.
They were happy I was in temporary distress.
When I close my eyes, I can rest.
They were plotting on how to keep me down.
God told me not to make a sound.
When they look in the mirror, they do not like what they see.
They need to ask God to come in and set them free.
God allowed me to see.
Every one of them betrayed me.
They were putting on false faces.
They were going to different places.
They pretended to have my best interest.
I discovered they were selfish.
People are not what they seem.
They are living false dreams.
Do not give an invitation if you were not sincere.
One thing I know God is always near.
They did not think I would be still standing.
God allowed me a perfect landing.
God sits high and looks low.
They will answer to him and this I know.
False faces seem to follow me no matter where I go.

33 FAMILY

A family should be about sharing relationships.
A family should not be hypocrites.
A family should be unconditional love.
A family sent from God above.
A family should be more than just having a baby.
A family should be respecting that man or lady.
A family should be passing on wisdom to the next generation.
A family should not be seeking their own sensation.
A family is supposed to be blood thicker than water.
A family is supposed to love you when you do not have a quarter.
A family knows right from wrong.
A family should be someone you can count on.
A family is unity.
A family is a community.
A family should not abuse.
A family is not your choice to choose.
A family should be there whether you win or lose.
God gives family advice.
God has paid the ultimate price with sacrifice.
God gave his son's life.

34 FINDING MY WAY IN THE UNIVERSE

I broke that generational curse.
I was told I could not do this or that.
Now all the haters want to chat.
I learned a long time ago.
Others opinion do not stop the show.
I had to find my own way.
I do not care what others say.
I kept my chin up.
Never give up no matter what.
The universe is so large.
God is the only one in charge.
I was taking jobs so I could survive.
It helped me stay alive.
God was the only one who knew.
What I was born to do?
I had my share of trials and tribulations.
God gave me the revelations.
I looked within my soul.
I must discover my way before I got old.
Everyone I trusted showed me his or her worse.
I found my way through the universe.
God removed the curse.

35 FRAGILE HEART

The heart is the lifeline to the mind, body, and soul.
Please stop treating my heart so cold.
The heart is precious as gold.
You must shape and mold it.
You cannot break it.
It is so delicate.
You must not abuse it.
You can lose it.
Life challenges could make it hard as stone.
You will find yourself alone.
You cannot without the heart live.
It allows you to give.
You must protect it; like a newborn baby.
You cannot open the heart to just any man or lady.
It beats fast when you are excited and slow when you are sad.
It sometimes yearns for a mother or dad.
Are you going to donate your beat per minute?
Are you going to make sure God is in it?
Someone woke up this morning in need of a heart.
This heart is a gift from God.

36 FREEDOM

Freedom is not to worry.
Freedom gives God all the glory.
Freedom chooses your mate.
Freedom decides your fate.
Freedom is a peace of mind.
Freedom does not care about a dime.
Freedom loves unconditionally.
Freedom makes decisions consciously.
Freedom is in God's will.
Freedom does not chase cheap thrills.
Freedom released from mental bondage.
Freedom does not take anyone hostage.
Freedom flies like a bird in the sky.
Freedom speaks the truth and not tell a lie.
Freedom is you and I am me.
Freedom sets us free.
Freedom is the choices you must make.
Freedom gives life and not take.

37 FRIENDSHIP

Friendship is to be treasured.
Friendship cannot be measured.
Friendship is not disloyalty.
Friendship is like royalty.
A friend sticks closer than a sister or brother.
A friend is not your father or mother.
A friend would be with you to the end.
A friend has shown me more love than my kin.
A friend would be with me through thick and thin.
My friend cares for me.
My friendship grows like a tree.
My friend would have my best interest.
A real friend will survive the test.
A friend is more than a trip to the mall or Monday night football.
A friend is there to pick you up when you fall.
They do not know the meaning of friendship.
They already slipped.
I found it very funny.
They were with me when I had money.
Friends should admit.
Friendship is a lifetime commitment.
They could not see.
God revealed them to me.
A friend is respect and love.
A true friend is from heaven above.

38 GENERATIONAL CURSES

I broke that generational curse.
Everyone I loved showed me his or her worse.
God gave me the key.
They could not see what God was doing through me.
I was never a nuisance to anyone.
They treated me like the prodigal son.
I was cursed by alcohol, drugs, and rape.
God helped me escape.
They hated me for no reasons. It lasted for a few seasons.
God kept me strong and standing tall.
God protected me from them all.
I used to think it was a black thing.
No matter where I went, it was the same old thing.
People afflicted by jealousy.
They wanted to be me.
Some of them inherited this disease.
God says they must fall on their knees.
I treated others, as I wanted to be treated.
God did not allow me to be mistreated.
I did not ask to come from this seed.
They were filled with greed.
God supplied all my needs.
How did I get rid of this curse?
I had to put God first.
I forgave those who displayed their worse.
I kept my eyes on God and allowed him in my heart.

39 HATERS

Hater-Helpless Anger Towards Everyone Regardless
You should not be a hater.
You should try to be greater.
You must find your own way.
Ask God and hear what he has to say.
How you treat others are an expression of how you feel about yourself.
Hate is the number one cause of death.
There is a deep dark secret hidden beyond the surface of your being.
You or your parents were not able to be seeing.
It allowed you to lash out at others.
It starts with the relationship you had with your father or mother.
Hate is something that is taught.
Hate can be bought.
It could be a total stranger.
That could help you out of danger.
God will help you with your anger.
It may be unresolved feelings on the inside.
That is displayed on the outside.
It was good that you were afflicted.
Now you can rid yourself of any addiction.
There is help for you.
You can be true. It is forgiving others who may have hurt you.
You are not alone. God is on his throne.
You will see once you are clean within.
You will be happy in your skin.

40 HAUNTED BY MY PAST

Haunted by my past, God told me it would not last.
No, matter what I did in my life.
There was always someone stirring up strife.
I forgave you and myself.
You need to let my past stay on the shelf.
I tried to stay away from that dark place.
Every time I turn around someone is throwing my past in my face.
They just want to take my place.
I reflect on what they can become.
I could not have done it without his only begotten son.
All I hear I remember when.
We all committed sin.
I know you have a skeleton in your closet.
You just do not have the courage to reveal it.
You tried to seal it.
Who are you to judge me?
You are not the one who set me free.
Yes, I did things I am not proud of.
God forgave me and sent his divine love.

41 HOW COULD IT BE?

How could it be a person hates without a cause?
How could it be? He or she wants what never was.
How could it be the earth is not here to stay?
How could it be people kill each other every day?
How could it be someday it will end?
How could it be people and nations will not become friends?
How could it be there is nowhere to run or hide?
How could it be God is the only one on our side?
How could it be no matter what color, race, or creed?
How could it be when that day comes, we must pay our deeds?
How could it be something everyone is afraid of?
How could it be? God is the only one we can love.
How could it be?

42 HUMAN SHIELDS

I used him as a human shield to hide my pain.
He kept me out of the rain.
God kept me sane.
It was very difficult to reveal my heart.
I would only talk to God.
I was hurt so many times by my race.
I could not remove the pain from my face.
I wonder who else made a fuss about one of us.
God was the only one I could trust.
The man could not understand my heartaches as a child.
The relationship lasted for a little while.
There were so many things on my mind.
The man could not read the signs.
Every time I found myself in one hot mess.
God advised me. It was only a test.
I seek God to guide me through.
This is my story what about you.
I must be true.
It keeps me from being blue.
I had to fall on my knees.
God has given me the keys.
I had to yield.
God set me free from the human shield.

43 HUMANITY

We are one race.
We are humans.
We need to love their neighbors as they love themselves.
We need to get our children off welfare.
People need to stop compromising what is right.
People need not give up without a fight.
People poisoned their children with this illusion about life.
They sit back and watch them kill each other with a gun or knife.
Parents forgot things they had done at their age.
They sit back and say they are going through a stage.
What has this generation been reduced to?
God cannot do it without you.
People lost sight of their future.
Some of them were deprived of nurture.
People concerned more about themselves.
God's word needs to be back on the shelves.
People need to break that generational curse.
Things will never get better only worse.
People tried everything on their own.
They left with broken homes.
People need to get back on God's throne.
Life destroyed without the presence of God.
People need to love God with all their heart.

44 HUMILIATIONS

The adversaries could not be seeing.
Humiliation was layers of my skin removed from my being.
I was at a low point in my life.
Every one of them displayed nothing but strife.
I swallowed my pride.
God was the only one on my side
It was such a disgrace.
I ended up in their place.
They took my humbleness for granted.
Some of their souls were contaminated.
I was embarrassed to say they were my friend or kin.
They were buried in their own sin.
My eyes were filled with tears: for so many years.
God elevated me on so many levels.
I had never seen so many devils.
I fell on my knees.
God made me strong as trees.
They tried to revolt against me.
The blood of God covered me.
Humility leads to greatness.
They were full of sadness.
God says it was only a test.
God allowed me to do my best.
Humiliation brings about elevation.
It was worth it in the end.
God allowed me to win.

45 I AM HAPPY IN MY SKIN

I am happy in my skin.
God validated me from within.
I was bullied as a child.
It made me run wild.
I was called everything but the child of God.
Beauty is what inside of my heart.
Good looks can be bought.
Real beauty must be taught.
Attractiveness is in the eye of the beholder.
Beauty will not be with you when you get older.
Bullies ugly words use to cut like a knife.
I did not fall into their trap of strife.
Beauty is not what you see.
Beauty dwells inside of me.
Beauty is meant to be.
I did not believe the lie.
God will be with me until you die.
Beauty must be happy in its skin.
Beauty does sin.
God can help beauty if it lets him in.
I will be true to the end.
I am happy in my skin.

46 I CRIED OUT AND HE HEARD ME

I cried out and he heard me.
When I was about to die; God told me not to believe the lie.
Family and friends had forsaken me: God awakened me.
I looked in the mirror and hated what I had seen.
God gave me that gleam.
I had not experienced Gods divine love.
It was sent from heaven above.
Others were offering me a hit.
God rescued me from that bottomless pit.
God told me not to worry or cry.
He will be with me until I die.
When my self-esteem was low, God took over the show.
God taught me to take it slow.
While jobs and promotions past me by:
family and friends began to lie.
They thought I was going to fall.
God protected me from them all.
When I had no place to live, God made my enemies give.
God opened doors that no one could.
God made my enemies my footstool.
I wanted it so fast. God showed me it would not last.
I broke that generational curse.
Everyone I trusted showed me his or her worse.
I hated what I become.
God sent his only begotten son.
I heard about God.
I did not know him for myself.
I told God I would not trade him for anyone else.

47 I FORGIVE YOU

Forgiveness was very difficult to do.
When I was mistreated too.
The betrayals and deceit were hard to digest.
I had to get so many things off my chest.
I looked into the enemy eyes.
I saw nothing but lies.
God's grace and mercy pardoned my sins.
Forgiveness starts from within.
God crucified my enemies.
They were nothing but want to be's.
Clemency must take place if I want to finish the race.
I will never forget. I must forgive if I want to live.
Forgiveness is the largest act of kindness.
Forgiveness allowed me to rest.
I must leave it in the past: if I want to last.
To forgive people who did me wrong.
It released to make me strong.
My conscious is clear. God is always near.
He wiped away every tear.
It was all right. I was not up at night.
I would not give the enemy the pleasure to return evil for evil.
It is the trick of the devil. God elevated me to the next level.
It is a great feeling to be free and not have hatred in my heart.
I know that is a true blessing from God.

48 I HAD TO BE MYSELF

I do not care about what anyone thinks.
I had never seen a shrink.
It was not a difficult task.
Once I removed the mask
Everyone would ask. Would I last?
They wanted to know if I had it together.
God protected me in any kind of weather.
I could not be transparent with anyone.
God was the only one.
They could not handle the real me.
They would judge me.
I was planted as strong as a tree.
Layer by layer I was uncovered.
It was so much they discovered.
God allowed me to remove myself from the shelf.
Now I know how to be myself.

49 IDENTITY CRISES

Who am I really?
I lost myself in the shuffle.
I had to be a mother for my sisters and brothers.
I had to be a maid and cook. It made me take a second look.
They could not see; what they had done to me.
A child was taking care of a child. It made me run wild.
They were on the outside looking in. They were getting under my skin.
Who am I really?
American dream gets married, have children and live happily ever after.
That is a myth everyone I know it led to a disaster.
My life did not turn out the way I expected. I refused to accept it.
I know what I was born to do. No one guided me through.
I was taking jobs to survive. God was the only one on my side.
Who am I really?
I do not know, but others tried to tell me so.
No matter what situation I found myself in.
God told me it was not the end.
I knew I did not belong. Everyone was treating me wrong.
They did not care about what I did.
Everyone tried to treat me like a kid.
They were so lost. They did not know the cost.
Who am I really?
I spent time finding myself. I removed my bible from the shelf.
I did not respond to them lashing out at me.
I was standing strong and tall as a tree.
It was so sad to be among so many haters. It made me want to be greater.
I played by the rules. They ended up looking like fools.
It was a fight with my past and future. I was never nurtured.
So here, I am with this dilemma, who is Emma?

50 IDLE MINDS

Idle mind causes an inactive body and soul to exist.
An idle mind has a risk.
An idle mind is not truly living.
An idle mind does everything willingly.
An Idle mind does not deposit anything in your life.
An Idle mind keeps up all kinds of strife.
Time is the most asset.
Idle minds do nothing but chat.
Time cannot be given back.
You must be careful about how you use it.
An idle mind will abuse it.
There is a time to be still.
The enemy job is to kill.
No sense of purpose creates an unoccupied space.
Do not let the enemy put you on a chase.
An idle mind is a room for failure.
God is the only one who cares about you.
God word is the truth.
God saved me during my youth.
An idle mind must be true.
God cannot do it without you.
An idle mind is so lost.
God paid the cost.

51 IMMATURES

I was chasing a ghost.
It was not clear to most.
I was spoiled rotten.
Anything I wanted I had gotten.
I thought the world revolved around me.
God was the only one who let me see.
I was being shattered with material things.
The Bible says, "I was a child. I spoke as a child.
I became an adult I put away childish things."
God had taken me under his wings.
It was like running after a rabbit.
It took a minute to break that habit.
I took myself out of the equation.
Therefore, God removed the abrasion.
I could blame it on this or that one.
I take full responsibility for what I had done.
I know I have won.
I could not make it without God's only begotten son.

52 IMPERFECTION

Everyone has some flaws.
It does not matter who you are.
God kept me from falling.
I found my true calling.
God does not put limits on my potentials.
He developed my credentials.
The blots were to make me aware.
God is the only one who cares.
It was time for me to face my deficiencies.
Therefore, I can turn them into testimonies.
God washed my blemishes clean.
No one could see I was steamed.
I had it covered up on the outside.
The real issues were on the inside.
I had to stop and look at myself.
I could not blame anyone else.
So, I could become true.
God guided me through.
It does not matter what I did.
God forgave me of my sin.
It was not my fault that I was afflicted.
God gave me a one-way ticket.
I did not ask to come here. God kept me near.
He knows every tear that I shed.
That is why he sent his son to die and bled.

53 INSTITUTIONALIZED MENTALLY

Prisons took their mind.
They served their time.
Some of the convictions did not fit the crime.
They are not prepared for society.
They returned to prison quietly.
Prisons destroyed families.
Prisons separated communities.
Prisons are not the answer.
Prison convictions are killing faster than cancer.
Prisons were built on man selfish gains. It drove some insane.
Billions of dollars spent on these bars.
Money used wisely could go very far.
Prisons are a way of intimidations.
Prisons put people on plantations.
It takes men and women working together.
This will make our country better.
We must come together as a nation. This requires dedication.
America economy reached an all-time low.
God was not a part of the show
We are wondering why things are not what it seems.
Some people gave up on their dreams.
Ten Commandments were enough to put fear.
God removed out of the equation and we shed only tears.
It kept most of them from doing wrong.
God's word kept this country strong.
We printed in God We Trust on our bills.
God is not very thrilled.

54 JOY-JUST OFFER YOURSELF

Life is a test.
Joy brings the world happiness.
Joy allowed me to get everything off my chest.
Joy allows me to do my best.
Joy gives me peace within.
Joy keeps me from committing a sin.
The birth of a child brings a person joy.
It could be a girl or a boy.
Joy is the first thing a child sees is his or her mother.
Joy does not need approval from others.
I was dealt with several bad hands.
God says. I can accomplish anything in this land.
God has a master plan.
God gives me joy.
God does not destroy.
God offered himself.
Joy is. Just offer you.

55 LEECHES

Leeches attached themselves for the wrong reasons.
They seemed to last only a few seasons.
They pretended to have my best interest.
They failed the test.
Some of them were put to rest.
They could not handle the long trip.
They abandoned ship.
I am glad they did.
I do not have to give them a gig.
Why do people attach themselves to you?
They will never be true.
They had their own hidden agenda.
God did not send them.
I did not comply.
They started to lie.
They fell off like flies.
God was the only one on my side.
He revealed them one by one.
Now, I look around there is none?
I am so happy the leeches are gone.
I do not have to sing a sad song.
I want people in my space to accept me for who I am.
They do not have run a scam.
They must be in the spiritual realm.
They must not be concerned with what I can give them.
True family and friends are more valuable than any gem.

56 LIES

Lies do not get you anywhere.
It makes you swear.
You tell one after the other:
before you know it, you are looking for another.
So, stop trying to be a hero.
It makes you a zero.
Are you living a lie?
Can you really testify?
You can start by facing the lie.
You cannot overcome it until you try.
Why you cannot take off your mask?
Is it a difficult task?
Will you remove your bible from the shelf?
Are you concerned about anyone else?
Can you be honest?
Are you just being modest?
When are you going to change these lies into the truth?
Do you think these lies have robbed you of your youth?
It does not matter what lie you are living in.
You must search for the truth within your being.
This will stop you from sinning.
God can help.
God cannot do it without you.
It starts with you being true.

57 LIFE

Life is a mystery.
God is history.
I heard so many stories.
God gets all the glory.
To live or die is not up to a man.
Man will swift you like sand.
My existence baffled some.
I am here and others are gone.
Life is not to be taken for granted.
Some of them wish they could be candid.
My way of life has opened many doors.
Please respect my life the way I respect yours.
I had to learn as I go. God is in control of the show.
Time is on my side. God is the one who guides.
Life comes with limited days.
I must give God all the praise.
I am human in a vacuum consumed by life tribulations.
The pure in heart can see God's revelation.
Life is worth living.
I had to fill my heart with giving.
No matter how hard life problems may seem.
God's love guides me through the stream.
There was a time in my life I thought I was alone.
God was there all the time sitting on his throne.
He was waiting for me to open my heart for his divine love.
That was sent from heaven above.

58 LIFELESS

She had lain lifeless in that bed for so many years.
Whenever I would visit her, it brought me to tears.
How could you do that to her?
You know who you are madams and sir.
She made so many sacrifices for all of you.
It was something so simple you could not do.
Every one of you should be a shame of yourself.
There is no excuse for what you have done.
God will redeem you with his son.
She cried out for help.
You could not think of anyone but yourself.
I did everything I could to save her life.
You created a lot of strife.
I would not wish that on my worst enemy.
You have the audacity to call yourself family.
She was already thin.
You allowed her to evaporate out of her own skin.
I know this will be true.
God will take care of you.
I forgive you for what you have done, but I will never forget.
God's grace and mercy cleared my conscious of any regrets.

59 LEAVING AMERICA

America is the land of the free and the home of the brave.
I was treated like a slave.
America judged me based on the color of my skin.
My own people lost their heritage and next of kin.
Someone died so I could be free.
God's grace and mercy guided me.
Hatred and racism are so prevalent.
Other countries make us irrelevant.
America lost its way.
People killed every day.
Babies having babies, and no one seems to care.
You voice your opinion. You are giving the evil stare.
America did not expect this country to be where it is today.
People who have degrees cannot earn their pay.
God has the last say. We must start to pray.
America is so corrupt. America does nothing but fuss.
America does not know who to trust.
America is a bad dream.
America is not what it seems
America is wealthy for everyone to get a piece of the pie.
You cannot take it with you when you die.
America let Americans down.
America allowed hatred to turn this country upside down.
I traveled to other countries.
They respected my pedigrees.
I was treated like a queen.
America is a unique civilization.
America must put God back in the equation.
America supposed to be the home of the free and the brave.
America was never meant to be the home of the slave.

60 LIVING IN A WORLD OF CONFUSION

I was living in a word of confusion.
I thought it was an illusion.
The world looks at life as a game.
Everywhere I went the problems were the same?
The babies were crying.
The people were dying.
The world lost control.
Some of them were caught up with drugs, sex, and rock in roll.
The people were being used.
The children were being abused.
When will it ever stop?
No one seems to know.
God is the only one who can stop the show.
The enemy paints this delusion.
God is not the author of confusion.
God is love.
It is sent from heaven above.

61 LIVING WITH THE ENEMIES

God revealed this to me.
I did not know. I was living with enemies.
They were full of emptiness and bitterness.
I showed them nothing but kindness.
I was living with strangers.
God protected me from any dangers.
They gave an invitation to come and stay with me.
I thought I was planted like a tree.
Little did I know; I was told I had to go?
I knew my funds were very low.
Therefore, I packed my bags and headed out the door.
I made a promise never no more.
I would not ever live with anyone.
God sent his only son.
I would rather sleep on the streets.
Before, I allow myself to be betrayed by deceit.
You know who you are. You will not get very far.
What did I ever do to you?
I was nothing but true.
It made me realize you are so empty inside.
You perpetrate on the outside.
I forgive you. You are in spiritual darkness.
You allowed your heart to feel nothing but hardness.
You claimed to be a child of God. It was only a façade.
You do not have a Godly relationship.
You revoked your spiritual citizenship.
My prayer is for all of you.
You will one day be true not to me but you.
God is the only one who can heal you.
You must allow him to.

62 LOYALTY

Loyalty is a lifestyle.
Loyalty does not crush your smile.
Loyalty is someone I can trust.
Loyalty does not throw me under the bus.
Some does not understand what this concept means.
I could not believe what my eyes were seeing.
Loyalty is a true friend.
Loyalty comes from within.
Loyalty sticks closer than any kin.
Loyalty is a mutual agreement.
Loyalty knows how to handle a disagreement.
Loyalty is being true to the game.
Loyalty does not drive you insane.
Loyalty is royalty.
Loyalty is not infidelity.
Loyalty is to death do us part.
Loyalty does not break your heart.
Loyalty comes from God.

63 MAKING THE RIGHT DECISION

Making the right decisions were hard to do.
I did not have anyone to guide me through.
I had some hard decisions to make.
I was pressured into many mistakes.
I had to look within myself.
I could not depend on anyone else.
God let me know.
It was the right way to go.
I had a fight.
The decisions had to be right.
I was tempted by sex and drugs.
God sent his divine love.
God could not do it without me.
I decided to let God set me free.
I refused to make the same mistake twice.
It had almost cost me my life.
God's son already paid the price.

64 MIND GAMES

Mind games are the same.
No matter where you go.
Everyone is trying to put on a good show.
Some of them are fast and others are slow.
The battle is in their mind.
It did not cost them a dime.
It is only a matter of time.
They will trip on a land mine
Mind games are being quiet.
I was on autopilot.
They thought I was a dumb blonde.
I played right along.
It made me very strong.
They could not read my mind.
I was with them all the time.
They did not know.
I was going to let them go.
I was so upset.
This game was not over yet.
They thought I was their pet.
They tried to use and abuse.
They were going to lose.
I was so naive to believe.
They were on my side.
God was my only guide.
They enjoyed playing mind games.
It will eventually drive them insane.

65 MISERABLE WITHIN ONESELF

Your behavior is so unpredictable.
You try to make everyone around you miserable.
When I look into your eyes, all I see is so many lies.
Your eyes say who you are.
With this type of personality, you will not go very far.
I see your heartache and pain.
If you do not change your behavior, it will drive you insane.
Your heart aches for love.
It is sent from heaven above.
Why do you do what you do?
When everyone that loves, you are trying to help you.
Because you hate yourself, you do not want love from anyone else.
Your eyes were filled with sorrow and pain.
Ask God to help you change!
Things do not have to be this way.
Why do you say what you say?
God is peace and love.
God is true happiness from above.
When the storms in your life ceased, you know you have peace.

66 MONEY CANNOT BUY LOVE

Money cannot buy me, love.
Love is sent from heaven above.
No one can put a price on it.
That is why so many quit it.
I faced it: in order to embrace it.
I did not realize I was buying love: until I was, broke.
It was a joke. They were around for the wrong reasons.
Some of them lasted for only a season.
If I was doing the buying, no one was lying.
It was a horrific experience to know my money bought love.
It was my family and friends.
They were the ones who had done me end.
I was looking for love in all the wrong places.
I saw so many faces.
When I think about the times, they did me wrong.
They made me strong.
They thought they were on top of things.
God took me under his wings.
They are in mental bondage.
God is the only one who can set them free.
If you do not believe, then look at me.

67 MULTIPLE PERSONALITIES

I do not know who you are.
You must be bipolar.
You have the signs and symptoms.
God can help you eliminate them.
You depressed, sleepless, hopeless, and suicidal.
God should be only idle.
I tried to give you my shoulder.
You did nothing but treat me colder.
You do not want anyone to get closer.
You are out of control.
The enemy consumed your soul.
This is what I was told.
You change your mood every minute.
God is not in it.
You say one thing and do another.
You were nothing but trouble.
Where did this personality come from?
God sent his only begotten son.
You can peaceful during the storm.
God's love will keep you warm.
I know there is not a cure.
God can heal you for sure.
You must want him to.
God cannot do it without you.

68 MY LAST BREATH

As I sat waiting on the bus, I knew this was not someone I could trust.
A revolver pointed in my face.
I wanted to put him on a chase.
I did not know what to do.
I still did not have a clue.
Do you need a ride?
This is what he replied.
Little did I know?
I would be thrown to the floor.
I hit my head on the door.
Screaming and yelling was what I did.
I was just a little kid.
No one could hear my cry.
I knew I was about to die with his hands around my throat.
I was about to choke.
I felt my last breath leave my body.
I promised not to scream anymore.
He had let my neck go.
After he did what he wanted to me.
I was in a daze and could not see.
It is something I will never get out of my head.
I thought I was dead.

69 MY SOUL DELIVERED FROM DEATH

God delivered my soul from death.
This experience was better than wealth.
I was in a very dark place in my life.
God's son paid the price.
God brought me from a long way.
Sometimes I went astray.
I cannot explain it.
I will never quit.
What God called me to do?
I will be always true.
I cried out to God and he heard me.
God's love and mercy set me free.
God's loves to surpass all understanding.
God let me make a perfect landing.
God spared my life for a reason.
It is not for a season.
I should be dead and in my grave.
God is the only one who can save.

70 NO SENSE OF DIRECTION

There was one generation after another.
I was without a father or mother.
I did not understand.
How could I be swift like sand?
I felt as though I was from another land.
It was very difficult to reach me.
Therefore, I had to flee.
I realized life is not a game.
If I did not change, it would drive me insane.
It did not matter how well I performed.
No one prepared me to be on my own.
I knew it was something inside of me.
I had no one to bring it out of me.
It was in my brain.
I used this behavior to cover up the pain.
God could take me places no man could.
I just had to say I would.
I have now a sense of purpose and respect.
No one can take it away from me this I can bet.
The choice was up to me to be true to myself.
I would not trade God for anyone else.

71 OPTIMISTIC

It is good in every bad circumstance.
I needed a second chance.
Certain situations were only temporary.
I made God's word my sanctuary.
I was confident that God would bring me out.
I could not doubt.
God revealed with his spirit.
I kept God in it.
The enemy was using the flesh.
God reminded me it was only a test.
God kept me hopeful that brighter days were on its way.
All I had to do was pray.
Life had its way of dealing me a bad hand,
I had to be cheerful in this dark land.
I did not have the answers.
I did not allow life to consume me like cancer.
I was tired of being treated like pollution.
God's word was my solution.
I had to cry and persevere my way through life.
God's son has paid the price.
God was shaping and molding me for tough days.
I had to believe what his word says.
I looked back on my life.
God removed the strife.
God's grace and mercy protected and guided me.
I am truly free.

72 PAIN-Penetrating Anger in Negativity

Pain is when your heart was broken.
Pain is when not one word being spoken.
Pain is once you were hurt.
Pain is when you were treated like dirt.
Pain is after you gave your all.
Pain allowed you to take a fall.
Pain is that throbbing sensation that will not go away.
Pain is trying to survive it another day.
Pain is an ache. You cannot fake.
Pain is not being able to trust again.
Pain is not allowing it to drive you insane.
Pain is this big black hole.
The pain got inside of my soul.
Pain is looking for your enemy in the eye.
Pain knows when you were told a lie.
Pain smiles on the outside.
Pain deteriorates on the inside.
Pain moves beyond the injury.
Thank God, it did not require surgery.
Pain distinguishes between what is real.
Pain does not accept cheap thrills.
Pain takes it one day at a time.
Pain is not letting it rob you blind.

73 PEACE

Peace is in the mind.
Peace separates with time.
People can do to you only what you allow them to.
The person who brings you peace is you.
A peace that surpasses all understanding comes from God above.
The way to obtain this peace is through his love.
Peace can be around the world, in America, on your job or in the home.
Peace is spending time alone.
The battle is in your mind.
There is where you can find.
Peace, joy, and happiness
Peace will remove all the mess.
God will give you peace to pass the test.
Therefore, you can find your true self.
If you do not find peace, it will cause your death.
Love and harmony are the true meaning of peace.
If everyone loves, violence will cease.

74 PESSIMISM

I had my share negative people through my journey of life.
I did not let them give me any advice.
I saw many gloomy days.
God's word has the final say.
I had cynical people telling me what I could not do.
The adage is true.
Some people enjoy being blue.
I can do all things through God who strengths me.
God set me free.
I would never be anything. I used to hear.
God wiped away every tear.
I give God the glory.
Keep reading this book you will know the rest of the story.
Life is hard to do.
I believe what you put in the universe will come back to you.
Silence destroys a person more than anything
If you are not going to say good things, please say nothing.
I was bewildered by certain people behaviors.
I am grateful I have a savior.
I had to stay away from halfhearted people.
They will leave you crippled.
I will continue to keep hope alive.
God is the only one on my side.

75 POOR IS A STATE OF MIND

Poor is a state of mind. God did not charge a dime.
I am not poor in my mind or spirit.
I made sure God was in it.
I was homeless before.
My mind was not poor.
I was waiting for God to open the door.
Food is an essential part of life.
God sent his son to pay the price.
Some people preyed on the poor to get rich.
They throw their soul in a ditch.
We are the wealthiest country in the world.
We should be able to feed every boy and girl.
Poverty is based on material gain.
Poverty had driven some insane.
What would you want to accomplish on this universe?
You could learn a bible verse or break that generational curse.
Are you happy with where you are right now?
You want the universe to say wow.
Life comes with choices.
Do not listen to negative voices?
Remember poor is a state of mind.
You can change your situation with the flip of a dime.
It is up to you to be true. You make every second count.
God will bring you out.
God is the only one you will give an account.
You cannot do it without God.
You must allow him in your heart.

76 PRIDE

Pride is a form of sin. God cannot get in.
The heart of conceit produced nothing but deceit.
The smile on pride face shifted the blame.
Pride continues to play these games.
The problems were all the same.
The outside appearance was very deceiving.
Pride kept me from achieving.
I had no idea that pride was so self-absorbed.
Pride cannot handle my Lord.
I was living in a bubble.
God protected me from all types of trouble.
I was consumed by this vacuum of pride.
Words could not describe.
What was I feeling inside?
God was the only one on my side.
I had to look within.
Pride caused me to sin.
Pride was a soul of evil.
Pride was sent by the devil.
Pride gave this illusion.
God is not the author of confusion.

77 RACISM

Racism= Radical Against Colored Inherited Stupid Mindset
I could not get it out of my mind.
Racism hated by others and my own kind.
They displayed it all the time.
I did not choose the color of my skin.
It was so sad to say some of them were kin.
God made us one race.
It is humans.
God did see.
How they treated me.
It reflects how they felt about themselves.
God can help them and no one else.
They must face those demons they possess inside.
Man judges the outside.
God searches the heart.
Do you honestly know why you hate?
It could be from something you ate, betrayals, disappointments, or lies
Give it to God and he will turn your dark midnight into blue skies.
He cannot do it without you.
You must be true.
You must love God.
It is sent from heaven above.
You will experience his unconditional love.
It will be easy to share the love with any race.
God will provide you that special place.
You will be able to remove racism from your face.

78 RESPECT

God laws allow us to respect one another.
Respect is how you treat your father or mother.
Respect should be a given.
Respect comes from heaven.
Respect values one's opinion.
Respect does not have dominion.
Respect is earned and learned behavior.
Respect is our savior.
Respect is how you treat yourself.
Respect does not need to be validated by anyone else.
Respect produces what it sees.
Respect is not a tease.
Respect is what you say and do.
Respect must be true.
Respect is having respect for me and you.

79 RICH IN SPIRIT

Rich in spirit is worth more than gold.
This is what I was told.
Rich is not how much you possess.
Rich is giving God access.
Rich is satisfied in your being.
Rich is not what you are seeing.
Rich is not fancy cars and homes.
Rich is being ok with you when you are alone.
Rich can put on a show for the crowd.
Can you honestly say you are proud?
There is nothing wrong with acquiring material things.
Rich is when you allow the possessions to be your king.
If you were to die today, what would others say?
Are you living or existing with your wealth?
It will be giving to someone else after your death.
Rich is preparing yourself for when you get old.
Rich is happy in your mind, body, and soul.

80 SACRIFICE

The snakes do not know what it takes.
When you are trying to elevate all, they do is hate.
Sacrifice is to give up something to get something.
The haters never wanted anything.
They are where I left them many years ago.
Ask them where they are going, they do not know.
They never attempted to step out on faith.
They sit around day after day.
I did not even think twice.
Life comes with sacrifice.
I know what I was born to do.
God, I could not do it without you.
I put it on the shelf for so long.
God's love kept me strong and from doing wrong.
I accomplished things the snakes wish they could.
I took a stand.
I had to get what was mine in this land.
Before I would be, sift like sand.
I could not do it without Gods plan.
God is the only connection I need.
I did not have to pay any deeds.
God paid the price.
It was purchased with his life.
That is a real sacrifice.

81 SECRET ENEMIES

I did not know you were my enemy.
God revealed everything to me.
You were very clever.
You were sent by the devil.
You disguised so wisely.
God was always on my side.
I treated you with nothing but respect.
How could I ask for something you lack?
I trusted you.
You were not very true.
God advised me to trust no woman or man.
God is the only one with a plan in this land.
You swift me like sand.
God does understand.
You were both male and female.
You chose to send your soul to hell.
What you have done to me?
God was the only one who could see.
God set me free from my secret enemy.

82 SELF-ABSORBED

He was so full of himself.
He could not see anyone else.
Do not trust a smile. It will devour you like a reptile.
He was so self-centered.
I could not detect it before I entered.
He stared in the mirror all the time.
He did not have a dime.
He was so self-consumed. He was left doomed.
He tried to get his swag on.
He knows right from wrong.
He will end up alone.
He does not care where he dwells.
He does not know himself very well.
He is sending his soul to hell.
He has an ego so big.
He has several illegitimate kids.
He could not see his life had no beginning or end.
The enemy had him drowning in sin.
He could not see his future.
God is the only one who can nurture.
He was caught up in material things.
God was calling him under his wings.
He is a man that has a little boy inside crying to come out.
He was seeking the wrong clout.
God is the only one who can bring him out.

83 SELF EXAMINATION

How was I caught up in certain situations?
I had to give myself an examination.
I could not blame anyone else but myself.
For the choices, I made.
Most of the decisions were in Miami Dade.
Some of them were based on emotions.
It caused many types of erosion.
When I did not know what to do?
I relied on God to guide me through.
I could not lead myself.
God revealed my inner self.
I do not care what others think about me.
God set me free.
I steered myself astray; even to this day.
God leads me the way.

84 SELF-HATRED FREEWILL

How do you feel about yourself?
Is how you treat everyone else?
What makes you feel so sad inside?
You would torture yourself on the outside.
Whatever it is? GOD's love will get you through.
GOD cannot do it without you.
Stop trying to validate what others think.
You do not need to see a shrink.
If you love yourself, you will not be concerned about anyone else.
Love comes from GOD above.
Give it to him and he will show you his love.
You are what you eat: whether it is foods, cigarettes, drugs, or liquor.
GOD is the only one who can heal you quicker.
Self-love is so hard to do when you mistreated too.
Turn that hatred into love.
Your life will never be the same: because self-love is not a game.

85 SELF INFLICTED NARCOTIC (SIN)

Sin is a self-inflicted narcotic.
It made me psychotic.
I did it repeatedly.
Before I knew it, I was caught up in sin.
It did not matter what the addictions were.
I did not get very far.
It could be drugs, food, and alcohol, sex, gambling, or shopping.
There seems to be no stopping.
It was self induce.
It kept me from the truth.
I bought into the lie.
Sin will be with me until I die.
There was a way out.
I did not need any clout.
I wanted it for myself and no one else.
I did recover.
God is my father and mother.
It was a roller coaster ride,
It broke me down on the outside.
I could not do it alone.
I had to be strong.
Sin is a choice.
I had to listen to that still voice.
Some may take longer to heal.
SIN can no longer provide me that cheap thrill.

86 SELF PORTRAITS OF LOVE

Self-portrait of love is to love you.
It was not hard to do. I learned to be true.
It is an inward expression that will reach out to others.
Love was very hard with my mother.
I made excuses when I was a child.
I had to love myself for a while.
Love is the most powerful word in the universe.
Some used it as a curse.
Self-portrait of love, it is sent from heaven above.
Love is not selfish. Love is not breaking every dish.
Love cannot be bought. Love can be taught.
You must love with your heart.
It comes from God.
Love is not to be taken for granted.
Love does not walk away when you cannot stand it.
Love is not a one-way relationship.
Love is a partnership.
Love is holding hands in the rain.
Love is not driving each other insane.
Love is making each other smile.
Love is not having an illegitimate child.
Love is waiting for that special someone to share your mind, body, and soul.
Love does not leave you standing in the cold.
Love is not trying to be a star.
Love is a self-portrait of who you are.

87 Seventh Child

The seventh child was running wild.
It was very difficult to smile.
I was trying to fit in.
I committed all types of sins.
I came from a large family tree.
No one could ever see.
What they had done to me?
They brought me nothing but tears.
This took place for so many years.
I was the seventh oldest.
I was treated the coldest.
I remained true.
None of them had a clue.
It was a mentality draining.
It reminds me of Abel and Canning.
It made me very sad.
Some of them wanted what I had.
The enemy comes to destroy.
I could not be a kid playing with a toy.
I had to babysit while my parents were gone.
I could not wait to get out on my own.
I was seeking God's throne.
I knew I was different.
It was God sent.
Seven means fullness, completion, and perfection.
I thank GOD for revealing all the deceptions.

88 SEX-SELF EXPOSED XXX

Cheap thrills do not last forever.
Everyone is trying to be clever.
Sex is supposed to be for reproduction.
Sex is being used for seduction.
Sex is everywhere I go.
Sex is being exploited by everyone I know.
Sex is a beautiful thing.
Sex is neither right nor left wing.
Sex is baby having babies.
Sex is selling men and ladies.
Sex is overrated.
Sex is sophisticated.
Femininity and masculinity were discriminated.
Human sexual contents need to be educated.
Sex is for sale in the land.
Sex is exchanging bodily fluid.
Sex is everybody doing it.
Sex is not just for the heart.
Sex is a gift from God.

89 SHATTERED DREAMS

Shattered dreams are not what they seem.
It placed me back on a 9 to 5.
God was always on my side.
No matter how many sacrifices I made.
I found myself back being a slave.
I stepped out on faith.
None of them could understand my case.
It was not happening fast enough for them.
They abandoned me on a whim.
I refused to give up.
I asked myself and do what.
Some people are so mean.
God gave me my dreams.
They gave up on theirs.
None of them cares.
They wanted me to be like them.
Therefore, they try to crucify him.
I am reaching for the sky.
They began to lie.
No, matter what they say or do.
My dreams will come true.
My dreams may be deferred by not denied.
God is my guide.

90 SHELTERED

The enemy was sent to destroy me.
God gave me the key.
No weapon form against me shall win.
God wrapped his blood for my sin.
God gave me a favor.
They did not understand my savior.
No matter how far I strayed from him.
God was always near. He wiped away every tear.
I have special privileges that money cannot buy.
God promised to be with me until I die.
God secluded me from everyone.
It was his only begotten son.
While I was pondering, he had left them wandering.
Why he chose me and not them?
They were still running schemes.
God could not help them with their dreams.
God searches the heart.
I will never be apart.
A man searches the outer.
God searches the inner.
God saved me from being a sinner.
God placed me in his arms.
God protected me from any harm.
God sheltered me with his blood and his love.

91 SHOCK AND AWE

I was in shock with what I had to watch.
I was sifted like sand.
I will never place my life in anyone's hand.
It was not only a woman but also a man.
They could never understand.
I stayed out of their way.
I was very careful about what I had to say.
They know who they are and what they did.
I had to let them know I was not a kid.
When they did me wrong; God made me very strong.
They were not true.
They allowed their heart to get hard like glue.
This is what I was told.
It was about power and control.
They were warring within. Some of them were kin.
They committed all types of sin.
They were doing it for so many years.
They brought nothing but tears.
This ordeal has made me realize.
They were missing something on the inside.
They need to trust God.
It starts with the heart.
People will let you down all the time.
God's loves will be there, and it does not cost a dime.

92 SILENT ADVERSARIES

I had to learn when to be quiet.
Silent is a healthy diet.
The enemy could not beat.
My peace of mind no one could defeat.
My enemies tried to prove me wrong.
God made me strong; the calm after the storm.
God placed me in his arms.
God let me see.
They were out to destroy me.
They had no sense of direction.
God was my protection.
I had no choice. I had to listen to that still voice.
God did not allow the enemy to get in my way.
Therefore, I could hear what God had to say.
God is such a gentleman.
God revealed every one of them.
It was quiet when the wind blew.
They did not know.
God took over the show.
The enemy could not steal.
God kept my environment very tranquil.

93 SPIRITUAL DARKNESS

The disease can be defined as mental or physical illness.
You were told you have this sickness.
This bug you cannot shake.
It entered your body, mind, and soul like a snake.
You were told this ailment would consume your life.
You must tell your husband or wife.
It pierced your heart and made you cold.
Now you will not live to get old.
This malady turned family and friends away.
God allowed you to see another day.
Why do have to suffer in silence?
God is the one with guidance.
Diseases do not discriminate.
It terminates.
You can be up today and down tomorrow.
God's love will cover your sorrow.
The worse disease is spiritual darkness.
It clouded your mind with cerebral hardness.
No one can cure you of this syndrome.
God placed your infection on his throne.
You are psychologically and spiritually lost.
There is a cost.
It is more detrimental than any cancer.
Call on God and he will give you the answer.

94 STRENGTH THROUGH FAITH

Everyone treated me wrong.
It did not kill me, but it made me strong.
The power of God is the source.
I had no choice but to listen to God's voice.
There were times I wanted to give up.
God said enough is enough.
I was wounded by the pain.
God did not let it drive me insane.
God was always near.
God dried every tear.
God told me to hold on.
He will never leave me alone.
It was not my might.
God and I had become very tight.
The drive I have inside.
I had to put away my pride.
God gave me creativity.
God exposed my reality.
It was the Lord's vitality.
God paid my enemies for their ungodly deeds.
God's is all I will ever need.

95 SUFFERING IN SILENCE

No one should have to suffer in silence.
A miserable heart is full of malice.
Some people enjoy others pain.
They could one-day end up the same.
My pain is your sorrow.
We may not see tomorrow.
The worst suffering, I have seen.
God was not on the scene.
Have you ever suffered in silence?
I could never be balanced.
God has his own strategies.
No one knew what I was going through.
God was the only one true.
Some suffering could be justifiable.
They were some that were homicidal.
I witnessed so many deaths suffering in silence.
They did not want to be tormented: while they were dying.
There were those who were still lying.
I tried to rescue some of them from their distress.
Life is only a test. God decided to give them rest.

96 THE BRIGHT LIGHT

It was in my sight.
I had seen the bright light.
I was a child running wild.
I had known how to fake a smile.
Everyone died young.
I thought I was the next one.
A bullet caught in my rib cage.
I was enraged.
It missed my heart by two inches.
I ended up with stitches.
She wanted me dead.
That is what she had said.
Life and death are in the power of the tongue.
I was told I would be dead by one.
It was the devil playing with my head.
I was scared.
I have seen death at my door so many times.
Life is based on a roll of a dime.
The bright light was so clear.
I heard the voice of God very near.
He was standing down a long path:
with his hands extended inviting me to come.
I knew it was his only begotten son.
A still voice said to me.
It is not time yet.
I know the devil was very upset.
I was left here for a reason.
I did not know the season.
The bright light is so true.
The next time it could be you.

97 THE PAIN WILL STOP ONE DAY

No one could provide me with an easy solution.
I was treated like pollution.
Some of them started a revolution.
The pain over deaths and relationships will stop one day.
I did not know what to do or say.
Therefore, I had begun to pray.
I asked God would the pain stop hurting my heart.
The answer did come from God.
I must believe it in order to achieve it.
It was not easy to let go.
God controlled the show.
I had to stay on course.
It was God's choice.
God did not remove the pain.
God did not allow it to drive me insane.
No one could do it for me.
God revealed it to me.
It will go away someday.
This is what God had to say.
God gave me a peace that surpasses all understanding.
God says it will be a smooth landing.
I must be true to what I am feeling.
God is the only one who can do the healing.

98 THIEVES

Thieves come to rob you of your soul.
They do not care if you are young or old.
They have no conscious about their deceit.
They will knock you off your feet.
The soul is more precious than gold.
This is what I was told.
To have your person violated.
It is worst than being annihilated.
Why are some people so cruel?
I know they look like fools.
Thieves were robbed of their soul.
That is why they are so cold.
Thieves were victims of the same act.
That is why they go on vicious attacks.
I thank God for his mercy and grace.
God removed the thieves from my place.
You should have seen the look on their face.
I am glad it was not too late.
I did not allow my soul to get full of hate.
God allowed me to make it through with my fate.

99 TRAGEDY AFTER TRAGEDY

It was a tragedy with death.
It was a tragedy with wealth.
The tragedy was on the job.
God did not let me sob.
The tragedy was with family and friends.
The tragedy was nothing but sin.
The tragedy was with houses and cars.
God did not allow it to rip me apart.
The tragedy was happening so fast.
I asked God how long would this last.
This was a curse.
Everyone was at his or her worse.
I must confess.
God delivered me out of my mess.
God explained it was only a test.
God placed me under his blood
God gave me his love.
Life and death were in everything I say.
I thought I would never see a brighter day.
It was his only begotten son.
God showed me the victory was won.

100 TRUST

I was burned.
Trust must be earned.
Trust has many concerns.
Trust cannot be learned.
That was my biggest problem in life.
I trusted without any strife.
I was treating others, as I wanted to be treated.
Trust was not a part of their DNA.
I was their next prey.
Trust allows you to get from point A to B.
Trust is nothing you can see.
Trust is not saying one thing and doing another.
Trust believes your father or mother.
Trust seeks the truth.
Trust is so innocent like your youth.
Trust is not what you say.
Trust is what you do.
Trust is you or me.
Trust is as large as the sea.
Trust no one.
God says we must trust him and his son.
Why trust does not enter our heart?
Why we do not want to trust God?
Whom do you trust?
Trust God is a must.

101 TRUTH

The truth cuts like a knife.
It could hurt your husband or wife.
Can you handle the truth?
It is worse than removing a tooth.
I accepted the truth for myself.
I had to remove it from the shelf.
The truth set me free.
I opened my eyes and see.
It pierced my heart.
The truth comes from God.
It was my choice.
I listened to that still voice.
I was in denial for so long.
I made up my mind to be strong.
I know God would not lead me wrong.
No, matter who or what it is.
God knows his will.
For my life, the truth cuts like a knife.

102 UNITY

There used to be a unity in the community.
We allowed circumstances to divide us.
We do not know who to trust.
The love, respect, and harmony we use to have.
Other countries sit back and laugh.
We are not on one accord.
We seek everything and everyone, but the Lord.
We make promises we do not keep.
Some fell asleep.
We declared to be one union.
It is only an illusion.
The adversary separated us from our calling.
It allowed us to keep falling.
It is very frustrating to make a stand.
You find yourself alone in this land.
We disconnected from God, our country, family, and friends.
When will the madness end?
We must be willing to change.
Things will remain the same.
We must let go of the past.
Forgiveness will truly last.
We must forgive.
We must start where we live.
We made an agreement with God.
We would love each other with our heart.

103 VINDICTIVE SOULS

They were cruel on the job, in the home, church, and school.
The adversary made every one of them look like a fool.
Cruelty comes in many forms and styles.
It lasts for a while.
I had a question for God.
Why are there so many vindictive souls?
I will never forget what I was told.
Friction comes to destroy relationships, but peace intervenes.
It reveals things are not as bad as it seems.
God will take them under his wings.
Hostility is bitterness kept inside.
Discord was a part of their life.
It was between a husband and wife.
God is not the author of any rivalry.
God sent his only son to the cavalry.
God's word guided me through the rough times.
God did not charge me one dime.
God elevated me to another level.
I have never seen so many devils.
Why do people intentionally seek out to destroy a person's life?
God is the only one who can help them remove the strife.
When the blood shows up, the vindictive souls are gone.
God takes it to his throne.

104 VISION

Vision has provision.
God makes the final decision.
Visions were conceived today.
I did not care about what anyone had to say.
They were so caught up in yesterday.
Tomorrow is not here yet.
My visions had a lot of them upset.
I had to look beyond my current situation.
I continued my dedication.
They tried to destroy what God started.
They were so broken hearted.
God revealed the vision to me.
They could not see.
It was a mental picture.
They did not have a future.
God kept my focus.
None of them notice.
The enemy was nowhere in it.
God gave me his Holy Spirit.
Visions come from heaven above.
God sent his love.

105 WAR IN THE HEART

War in the heart, it is not sent from God.
Why are they stuck on stupid?
God knows who Cupid is.
I could not believe what my ears were hearing.
I could not keep my eyes from tearing.
The hatred was so strong.
Every one of them did me wrong.
I questioned my character.
Every relationship was a disaster.
I could not see what was thrown at me.
It chopped me down like a tree.
It brought me to my knees.
War in the heart is worse than any diseases.
I was mortified about so many enemies.
God's love was plenty.
It was seeing adults playing childish games.
None of them had any shame.
The backbiting, lying, and cheating were so prevalent.
It made me see they were irrelevant.
They were very clever.
War in the heart can only be of the devil.
It comes at any hour.
It seeks whom he may devour.
War in the heart
It is not a gift from God.

106 WHAT CLAN WAS I BORN IN?

They were trying to do me in.
Every one of them committed all types of sin.
I could not believe they hated me so much.
They could not embrace God's simple touch.
They do not know who God is.
They behaved like this for so many years.
They brought me nothing but tears.
None of them is living right.
They do nothing but argue and fight.
God is not in their sight.
They are filled with wicked hearts.
Who are these people I asked God?
God replied my lost flock that went astray.
They will come back one day.
This is what God had to say.
They must choose my way.
The truth and the light will set them free.
They must come through me.

107 WHERE I AM, IS NOT WHO I AM

Where I am, is not who I am!
I do not have to run a scam.
The words you say cuts like a knife.
I am not going to let you control my life.
I may not have what you have.
You wait and see do not laugh.
You have said I would not be anything.
You watch and see I will be a queen.
You just wait and see.
I can be whatever I want to be.
I will come out of this situation.
I will do it with my education.
Where I am, is not who I am!

108 WHO ARE THEY REALLY?

Every one of them was silly.
They said one thing, but they did another.
God removed the cover.
They tried to do me in.
They pretended to be my family and friend.
Evil comes from within.
They committed every type of sin.
They must find out who they are.
If they do not, they will not go very far.
I thought I knew who they were.
It made me question myself for sure.
There are not any perfect beings.
I could not believe what I was seeing.
It was like Dr. Jekyll and Mr. Hyde.
God was the only one on my side.
God can help them with their identity.
God ushered me into my destiny.

109 WHY DID I SURVIVE?

Why did I survive?
Most of my family and friends died.
I had to share my story.
Therefore, God could get the glory.
The enemy caused me heartaches and pain.
The enemy tried to drive me insane.
It made me wonder.
Why I did not go under?
I can speak only for myself.
Why did I survive death?
I had to pass the test.
God took the burden off my chest.
Now, I can finally rest.
I do not have to hide.
I could share my experience without any pride.
I know what I was left here to do.
It is not only for me but also for you.
It was time to be true.
Now, I know why I did survive.
God was the only one on my side.
I thank God for keeping me alive.

110 WISDOM WASTED

I believe some people are full of wisdom.
I experienced nothing but gruesome.
They reflected on their life, and they have nothing to show.
They lashed out on everyone they know.
These are people who live in the church.
They treated others and I like dirt.
They are glued to the bible.
They were worshiping idles.
Life should make you better, not bitter.
These people are very angry and quitters.
They displayed the victim mentality.
They lost sight of reality.
They do evil without thinking twice.
They gave up on life.
It took me numerous years to seek God's presence.
These people were not God sent.
Therefore, young people are so caught up.
The super saints display negative results.
They do not have long left on this earth.
They do not care about their worth.
When you reach a certain age; you should not be so enraged.
I believe some people can change.
These people are insane.
They know what is right and wrong.
God made me very strong.
They do things for good works: and not from the heart.
It is not pleasing to God.
They will pay one day.
God is watching what they do and say.

111 WOLVES IN SHEEP CLOTHING

Beware of false prophets who come in sheep's clothing.
They were not chosen.
Everything was stolen.
They are raven wolves.
They live in different neighborhoods.
They do not practice what they preach.
They produce only deceit.
Wolves come in different styles.
They hang around for a while.
They passed it on to their child.
The wolves come with a fake smile.
Telling me what they thought I wanted to hear.
Later I found myself in tears.
The child watches what they say and do.
The child does not know what is true.
Later to discover they were out to get you.
If you learn to listen, you will hear what you were missing.
Wolves can do only what you allow them to.
They will reveal themselves to you.
They were pretending for so long.
They do not know what is right or wrong.
Wolves in sheep clothing are counterfeit bills.
They are only cheap thrills.
They embezzle your body, mind, and soul.
They are so cold.
One day they will be old.
They will pay with their soul.

112 WORDS SMOOTHER THAN BUTTER

The words were smoother than butter.
It made me run for cover.
I did not see it coming.
It kept me running.
I believed everything they had to say.
God revealed the lies to me each day.
I had to hide.
God was the only one on my side.
You were both male and female.
The dishonesty will send them to hell.
You thought I was going to fall.
I listened to God's call.
God protected me from you all.
They tried to tell me what I wanted to hear.
Little did they know God was near.
Every time they had spoken.
I was given a token.
God let me see.
They were deceiving me.
God awakened me.
God will never leave or forsake me.
I will not fall for the words smoother than butter.
God set me free like no other.

www.ingramcontent.com/pod-product-compliance
Lightning Source LLC
Chambersburg PA
CBHW071455160426
43195CB00013B/2113